MYSTERY EXPLO

SEARCHING FOR

ATLANTIS

rosen publishing's
rosen central
New York

Barbara A. Woyt
and Ann Lewis

Published in 2012 by The Rosen Publishing Group, Inc.
29 East 21st Street, New York, NY 10010

First Edition

Library of Congress Cataloging-in-Publication Data

Woyt, Barbara A.
Searching for Atlantis/Barbara A. Woyt, Ann Lewis.
     p. cm.—(Mystery Explorers)
Includes bibliographical references and index.
ISBN 978-1-4488-4758-7 (library binding)—
ISBN 978-1-4488-4767-9 (pbk.)—
ISBN 978-1-4488-4775-4 (6-pack)
1. Atlantis (Legendary place) I. Lewis, Ann. II. Title.
GN751.W69 2012
001.94—dc22

                                                             2011000302

Manufactured in the United States of America

CPSIA Compliance Information: Batch #S11YA: For further information, contact Rosen Publishing, New York, New York, at 1-800-237-9932.

CONTENTS

INTRODUCTION

Atlantis. The very name is fascinating, conjuring up images of fantastic wonders and horrible disaster. The story is even more intriguing. It tells of an extraordinary country of great wealth and achievement in learning, engineering, science, and war. This land, the story continues, sank into the sea in a great cataclysm of fire and earthquakes in an area that people now refer to as the Atlantic Ocean.

Individuals have enjoyed stories about Atlantis for many, many years. That mystical lost civilization, the island of an ancient Golden Age, has spawned movies, television shows, novels, and comic books. In 2001 and 2003, the Walt Disney Studios even turned the story into animated features, entitled *Atlantis: The Lost Empire*, and its sequel, *Atlantis: Milo's Return*. But where does the original story of Atlantis begin? Is it based on truth?

Actually, the answer to the first of those questions, or at least a partial answer, comes from the ancient Greek philosopher Plato, who lived around 428 to 348 BCE.

Plato was the student of another great philosopher, Socrates, who lived about 470 to 399 BCE. Socrates was forced to take his own life when his teachings about forming an idyllic society started trouble with his government. Plato was sorely affected by his teacher's death, but very much influenced by

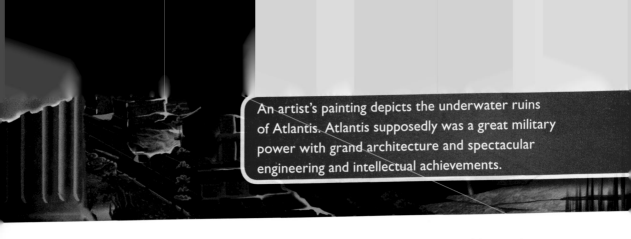

An artist's painting depicts the underwater ruins of Atlantis. Atlantis supposedly was a great military power with grand architecture and spectacular engineering and intellectual achievements.

his thinking. As a consequence, Plato continued his teachings, writing extensively on the ability of man to create a society that is good for all people. One of his works, *The Republic*, details the nature of justice and truth, the role of art in education, and how government should serve the people. He revealed his views through a series of fictional conversations he created between himself and several other philosophers, including his teacher Socrates.

Plato created fictional conversations like these in all his works, including the two books *Timaeus* and *Critias*, probably because he thought his teachings would be more easily absorbed by the reader this way. Because these books consist entirely of conversations, they are called dialogues, and it is in these two dialogues that he introduces the story of Atlantis. Plato wrote his dialogues around 355 BCE. Initially, he had intended to write a third dialogue, *Hermocrates*. The first part, *Timaeus*, focused on the creation of the universe and Earth. *Critias* told of Atlantis and its war with Athens. *Hermocrates*, the third in the trilogy, was supposedly going to describe Atlantis more thoroughly. The names of the dialogues refer to the three speakers, Timaeus, Critias, and Hermocrates, who are in the stories, along with Socrates. Scholars do not know why Plato stopped writing *Critias*, which was not finished, or why he never even started the dialogue *Hermocrates*.

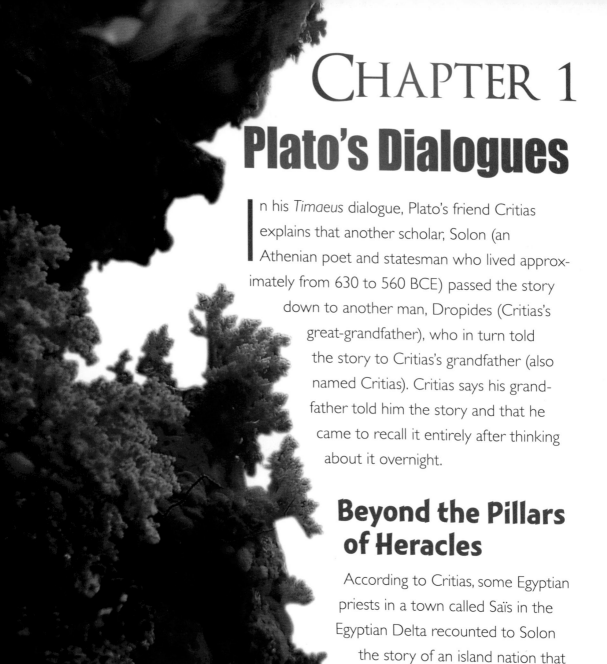

CHAPTER 1
Plato's Dialogues

In his *Timaeus* dialogue, Plato's friend Critias explains that another scholar, Solon (an Athenian poet and statesman who lived approximately from 630 to 560 BCE) passed the story down to another man, Dropides (Critias's great-grandfather), who in turn told the story to Critias's grandfather (also named Critias). Critias says his grandfather told him the story and that he came to recall it entirely after thinking about it overnight.

Beyond the Pillars of Heracles

According to Critias, some Egyptian priests in a town called Saïs in the Egyptian Delta recounted to Solon the story of an island nation that had once lain in the Atlantic Ocean, just beyond "the Pillars

ARGVMENTVM PLATONIS INDIALAGO
HYPARCI DELVCRI CVPIDITATE PERMARSI
LIVM FECINVM FLORENTINVM EXGRECO
INLATINVM TRADVCTVM :~

ROPOSITVM ł
PLATONIS IN
HIPPARCHO ł
EST DOCERE ʃ
NOS OMNES ᴚ
homineʃ bonum appetere cum &
illi qui propter auaritiam aberra
re uidentur bonum appetant il
li ʃiquidem lucri cupidi ʃunt: lu
crum utile eʃt utile uero bonū
itaɋ cupiunt. Et enim lucrum
damno contrarium. Damnum
uero cum obʃit malum: malo igitur contrarium. contrarium
malo bonum. lucrum igitur bonum. Quamobrem cum illi etiã
qui ab appetitu boni declinare uidentur: bonum cupiant nihil
iam repugnant quo minuʃ omneʃ homineʃ bonum appetant: bonū
autem duplex. Vnum finiʃ. Adfinem alterum. Illud propter ʃe
ipʃum. hoc propter aliud expetendum. Illius appetitio uoluntaʃ
huiuʃ electio illud uenerandum hoc utile: illo fruimur hoc uti
mur. Illiuʃ adeptio beatitudo: huiuʃ lucrum uocatur: lucrum
igitur eʃt boni utiliʃ acquiʃitio quod aduenerandi boni conʃe
cutionem conducere poteʃt. Quod uero ad hoc non confert nec
ipʃum utile eʃt nec eiuʃ adeptio lucrum. Laudanda igitur cu
piditas et omnibuʃ natura ineʃt Vituperanda autem opinio ꝑ
falʃa. que dum quod reuera
titum naturę adaduerʃa re
docet dum Socrateʃ definit
cri cupiditate refert. & ind
tur tamen Plato hac propoʃi
tanquam manifeʃta ad concludendum ꝗ omneʃ natura lucri

This page from a Latin manuscript of the fifteenth century shows one of the dialogues of Plato. Plato wrote about the fascinating story of Atlantis in his dialogues, around 355 BCE.

of Heracles." The Pillars of Heracles (called Hercules by the Romans) are the Strait of Gibraltar, a treacherous area of the sea beyond which the Greeks did not sail. Critias reports that this mysterious lost nation arrogantly tried to attack the cities in Europe and Asia and was held back. After that, violent earthquakes and floods destroyed it, and within a single day it sank beneath the sea.

In Plato's *Critias* dialogue, written later, Critias says something different from what he stated in the earlier dialogue. Instead of claiming to have heard the story of Atlantis from his grandfather (who heard it from Solon, who in turn had heard it from Egyptian priests), Critias states that his father had a manuscript on Atlantis, which he studied often as a child. This is only one of the many inconsistencies in the tale to surface. That, and the fact that the story was passed down by a friend of a friend of a friend, have caused scholars to scoff at the Atlantis legend for centuries.

Furthermore, that's not the only thing scholars don't like about the Atlantis legend. Another fault with Plato's story is when he says the destruction of Atlantis happened. According to him, the great tragedy occurred nine thousand years before he wrote the *Timaeus* dialogue. Yet the date that Plato gives for Atlantis would be far in advance of even the great civilizations of Egypt, the Near East, and India. In fact, according to known history, no civilization as advanced as the one that Plato describes existed so many thousands of years ago.

A Description of Atlantis

As stated by Critias, Atlantis was located in the middle of a series of concentric rings that alternated between rings of water and rings of land. The water

From space, an east-west view of the Strait of Gibraltar shows the gateway between the Atlantic Ocean *(bottom)* and the Mediterranean Sea *(top)*. Critias described the location of Atlantis as being in the Atlantic, on the other side of the Strait of Gibraltar, which the ancients called the Pillars of Heracles.

rings functioned as canals that also helped form a defense for the city. In the middle of the city, atop a mountain, stood palaces and temples. Poseidon, the Greek god of the sea, water, and earthquakes, ruled the land of Atlantis. Poseidon fell in love with a beautiful mortal woman, Clieto. Together they had five sets of twin sons, and each son ruled a section of the land. The people of Atlantis were said to have great gardens, splendid architecture, and amazing feats of engineering, from tunnels and bridges to race tracks and hot and cold springs. However, in due course, the people of Atlantis became greedy and dishonest. They invaded other lands, such as much of Western Europe and North Africa, intending to rule the world. Poseidon became enraged and destroyed Atlantis by unleashing earthquakes and floods, until the ocean devoured it.

A MIGHTY POWER

In Plato's *Timaeus*, Critias describes the island of Atlantis, according to what Egyptian priests had reported to Solon:

> Many great and wonderful deeds are recorded of your state [Athens] in our histories. But one of them exceeds all the rest in greatness and valor. For these histories tell of a mighty power which unprovoked made an expedition against the whole of Europe and Asia, and to which your city put an end. This power came forth out of the Atlantic Ocean, for in those days the Atlantic was navigable; and there was an island situated in front of the straits which are by you called the Pillars of Heracles, the island was larger than Libya and Asia put together and was the way to other islands and from these you might pass to the whole of the opposite continent which surrounded the true ocean.

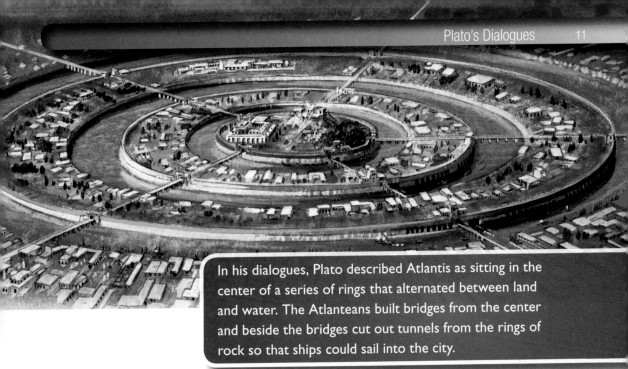

In his dialogues, Plato described Atlantis as sitting in the center of a series of rings that alternated between land and water. The Atlanteans built bridges from the center and beside the bridges cut out tunnels from the rings of rock so that ships could sail into the city.

Another theory that some researchers have introduced is that the place Plato called Atlantis influenced the birth of other great cultures, such as those of the ancient Egyptians and the Mayans of Central America. Although the mysterious place Plato called Atlantis died, survivors carried their culture to other places to start anew. This, they claim, would explain the mysterious way that cultures as far apart in geography and time as the Mayans and the Egyptians developed similar forms of architecture and science and how their cultures flourished in similar ways for thousands of years.

But could such a great civilization have existed so long ago yet influenced the great peoples and the civilizations of Egypt, Greece, and the Western world that followed? To answer this question, one has to look in more detail at when Atlantis is said to have existed and examine the problem of time.

CHAPTER 2

The Time Frame for Atlantis's Demise

In his writing, Plato sets the destruction of Atlantis 9,000 years before his telling of the story, which would make it approximately 9,500 BCE. This period is a problem to most archaeologists and scholars because as far as anyone knows, there were no civilizations of the type that Plato describes at this time. To give an example, this is three thousand years before the very first Pharaoh of Egypt!

Plato's Purpose

Perhaps, as some scholars believe, Plato deliberately exaggerated to prove a point, or to make his tale more mysterious or entertaining. This often happens, as stories get passed from generation to

In a page from a thirteenth-century Turkish manuscript, Solon *(right)* instructs some students. Many experts believe that Plato used the story of Atlantis's destruction to teach his students a moral lesson.

generation, much like a fish story in which the fish becomes larger and more fierce with each telling. Scholars feel that Plato embellished the story of the civilization to make it seem older and far more grandiose than it actually was. Some scholars believe that Plato used the destruction of Atlantis as a story to illustrate a moral or religious lesson.

THE ANCIENTS AND ATLANTIS

People did not believe that Atlantis truly existed until hundreds of years after Plato's time. The philosopher Aristotle, Plato's pupil, believed that Plato made up the story as a parable, or moral lesson, or to make a literary point. However, Aristotle's commentary (narration, or description) on the topic is now lost. Strabo (who lived from 64/63 BCE to 23 CE), a Greek historian, geographer, and philosopher, retold a comment that Aristotle made in which he said that Atlantis was entirely Plato's invention.

Plutarch (who lived from about 46 to 119 CE), a Greek biographer, believed that Atlantis was probably mostly fiction. He was inclined to believe that Egyptian priests had told Solon about a legendary island that had been swallowed up by the sea. Nevertheless, he also knew that Solon thought the tale was a good one because Solon had considered writing an epic poem about the lost Atlantis. Plutarch also wrote that Solon dropped the idea because of his increasing age and his worry that it would be too difficult a poem for him to write.

The Time Puzzle

One of the first to notice the problem of Plato's dating of Atlantis was a scholar named Immanuel Velikovsky (1895–1979), who proposed his theories in a book entitled *Worlds in Collision*, published in 1950. Velikovsky believed that Plato simply added "one too many zeroes" to his year count to exaggerate the age of the great nation. The island that Plato described, Velikovsky said, could very well have existed 900 years before Plato told the story, and to him this was the best explanation.

Not long after Velikovsky presented his ideas, Jürgen Spanuth (1907–1998), who studied theology and archaeology, started researching Plato's claim that the story of Atlantis originated in Egypt with Egyptian priests who told the story to Solon, who in turn passed the story to others. After studying Egyptian temple inscriptions and papyrus texts, he stated that Egyptians felt each month was in itself a "year," and so, counting up the months that would span back far enough in time, he would end up with 8,000 or 9,000 months ("years"). This would be the right time for the Egyptian priests to pass on the story, and for 900 years to pass before Plato could retell the story. Unfortunately, there's no real proof to support this idea.

Still others felt that Plato erred not on the side of exaggeration, but on that of underexaggeration. One such person was a Russian mystic named Madame Helena Petrovna Blavatsky (1831–1891). She believed, as did her followers, that Atlantis began to sink several million years ago, and completed its final descent into the ocean about 850,000 years ago—stating that Plato

Madame Helena Petrovna Blavatsky was a Russian mystic. She believed that Plato had misunderstood the date for Atlantis's sinking. She also thought that the Atlanteans' descendants built the Egyptian pyramids.

should have added a zero and made his figure 900,000 years ago. It would, she said, have been more accurate.

Later, German professor Albert Herrmann (1886–1945) stated that Plato's numbers were off by a factor of 30, and he manipulated the number to show that if one divided 9,000 by 30, the date could feasibly locate Atlantis in the place that he felt it should be, Tunisia.

With all this number stretching one can't help getting confused about when the destruction of Atlantis occurred. To combat this problem, many researchers simply avoided this puzzle entirely, deciding to look instead at where Atlantis might have been, rather than when.

CHAPTER 3

Atlantis: Fact or Fantasy?

Was Atlantis real, or was it a figment of Plato's imagination? There are many people who believe that Plato made up the whole story to prove a point. As a philosopher, Plato always came up with ideas of how society could be better, and he tried to convince his fellow human beings to follow those ideas. What, he wondered, would it take to create an ideal civilization, one based on a philosophy of wisdom and understanding?

The Size of Atlantis

To prove the theory that Plato made the whole story up, scholars point out that Plato's

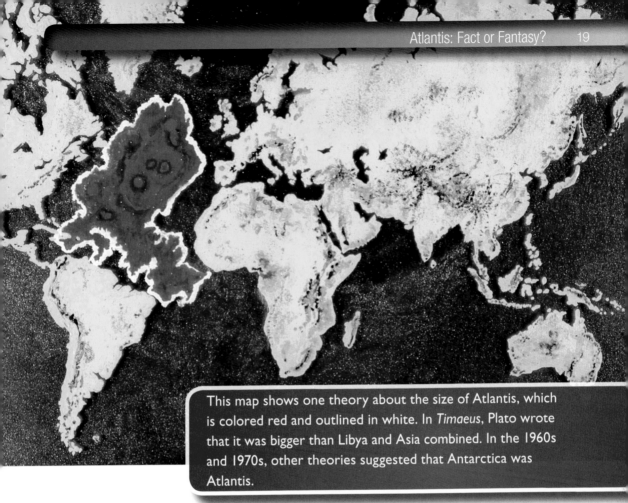

This map shows one theory about the size of Atlantis, which is colored red and outlined in white. In *Timaeus*, Plato wrote that it was bigger than Libya and Asia combined. In the 1960s and 1970s, other theories suggested that Antarctica was Atlantis.

description of Atlantis smacks of exaggeration. Plato says in his work *Timaeus* that "there was an island situated in front of the straits which are by you called the Pillars of Heracles, the island was larger than Libya and Asia put together."

The size of the island is almost too large to believe. How could such a large piece of land sink, never to be seen again? Most geologists find this to be absurd and especially deny that such an event could take place overnight or as quickly as Plato assumes.

Without Plato, No Atlantis?

Historians also note that no other author of Plato's time speaks of Atlantis. Surely if it had been a real place, historians or writers of other cultures would have mentioned the destruction of such a great civilization in earlier writings than those of Plato. Yet not even the ancient and widely traveled Greek historian Herodotus (approximately 484–425 BCE) mentions the story, and he, proceeding Plato by only thirty years, is reputed to have spoken to those very Egyptian priests who supposedly passed along the story to Solon. However, Herodotus wrote that the Phoenicians where the first Greeks to undertake sea voyages and that they were the first to pass the Strait of Gibraltar. It is believed that Plato knew of Herodotus's writings about these voyages and used that knowledge to help fashion his tale.

Plato's own student Aristotle states that Atlantis did not exist, but that the waters outside the Pillars of Heracles (the Strait of Gibraltar), where Atlantis

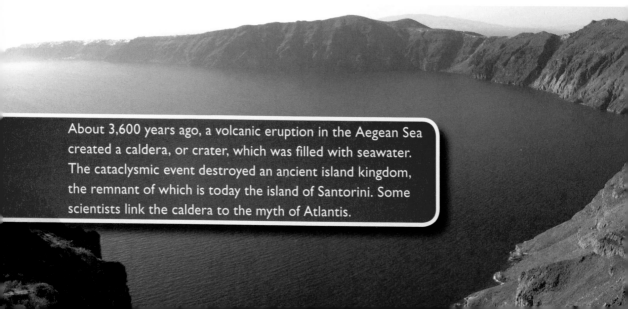

About 3,600 years ago, a volcanic eruption in the Aegean Sea created a caldera, or crater, which was filled with seawater. The cataclysmic event destroyed an ancient island kingdom, the remnant of which is today the island of Santorini. Some scientists link the caldera to the myth of Atlantis.

was supposed to have sunk, are strangely shallow. A couple of hundred years later, around 130 BCE, Plutarch (46 to 119 CE), another philosopher, said that Plato embellished the story originally passed to him to make it more of a fairy tale. It had, according to Plutarch, been a much simpler and more believable story at the outset.

Some Believable Claims

There are some, though, who feel that earlier stories do not exist because Plato gave the name Atlantis to a real place for which there was no known name, or at least not a name familiar to the Greeks. Could one of these ancient, nameless (at least to the Greeks) cultures be Atlantis? Some scientists think so, and many have stated theories of where and when such a culture may have existed. Another less scientific theory presents the mythical island of Mu in Asia, which stories say was also destroyed in a fiery cataclysm. Still others claim that locations such as parts of the Sahara were the ill-fated country.

In 1969, however, classical scholar J. V. Luce (1920–) made an interesting case for an element of truth to Plato's tale. In *Lost Atlantis: New Light on an Old Legend*, Luce makes a very sound argument that Plato's description of Atlantis, although embellished, could have been based on a very real story—the story of the great volcanic destruction of the Greek island of Santorini, an island near Crete. Apparently it is noted in Egyptian literature that all trade with Crete was suddenly cut off, and the story of the disaster was relayed to Egypt by way of sailors and survivors. Like the party game "telephone," where a

SANTORINI

The ancient name for the volcanic island of Santorini is Thera. Located in the southern Aegean Sea, southeast of mainland Greece, Santorini is what is left of a huge volcanic eruption during the Bronze Age that destroyed early settlements on what was once a single island. The volcano, called Thera, created a geological caldera that can be seen today. The volcano erupted about 3,600 years ago, during the peak of the Minoan civilization. The explosion, which could have created gigantic tsunamis, might have helped bring about the collapse of the Minoans on the island of Crete. Using studies that have been done on the islands of Krakatoa, Java, and Sumatra after the volcanic eruption there in early 1883 and the volcano's scale of destruction, some scholars believe that the waves that struck the Minoans on Crete were even more damaging. In *Lost Atlantis*, classics scholar J. V. Luce wrote:

> Upwards of 36,000 people perished within twenty-four hours on Java and Sumatra, and 290 towns and villages were destroyed . . . . I consider it a safe guess that the loss of life and damage to property were no less [on the island of Crete]. They may well have

been many times as great . . . . In addition to the effects of the blast and tidal waves . . . the hills and valleys of eastern Crete were covered to a considerable depth of ash fall-out.

Some scholars believed that the eruption of Thera during the Bronze Age had caused an island to sink into the ocean, exactly like Plato described in his dialogues concerning Atlantis.

story is passed and changed from person to person, Solon might have heard the story and passed it on to others, and eventually the tale could have landed with Plato. Luce concludes that the Minoan Empire of Crete in the sixth century BCE could very well be the basis for the story of Atlantis.

But even after Luce's theory was published, it didn't stop many scholarly—and some not so scholarly—people from letting their imaginations run wild with the story of an ideal world that had tragically come to an end.

CHAPTER 4

Some Theories About Atlantis

People from all walks of life have tried to uncover the secrets of Atlantis. Atlantean scholars come in the form of oceanographers, geologists, mystics, poets, archaeologists, sociologists, and even politicians!

What is it about this story that draws people of such different backgrounds to it? What conclusions have they reached, and how close to the truth are they?

Atlantis Was America

One of the first modern writers to look to Atlantis for inspiration was the English statesman, scientist, writer, and philosopher

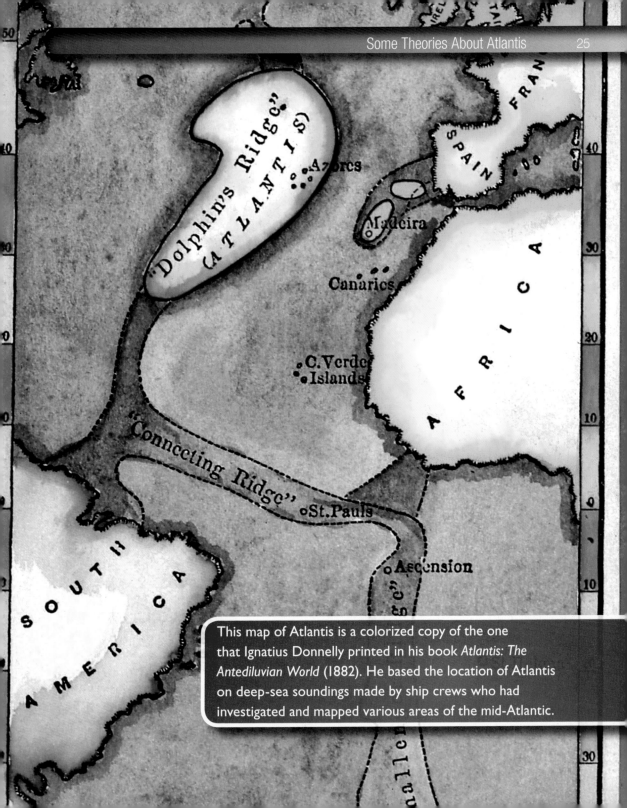

"Dolphin's Ridge" *(ATLANTIS)*

Azores

SPAIN

FRAN

Madeira

AFRICA

Canaries

C. Verde
Islands

"Connecting Ridge"

St. Pauls

SOUTH
AMERICA

Ascension

This map of Atlantis is a colorized copy of the one that Ignatius Donnelly printed in his book *Atlantis: The Antediluvian World* (1882). He based the location of Atlantis on deep-sea soundings made by ship crews who had investigated and mapped various areas of the mid-Atlantic.

Sir Francis Bacon (1561–1626). He wrote a fanciful tale entitled *The New Atlantis*, which placed the lost world in the New World of his time: America. In his story, some members of the Atlantean kingdom had survived the tragedy by building an ark and journeying across the waters to a new land they called Bensalem. Very few scholars consider Bacon's story to be more than a flight of fancy.

Some So-called Scientific Theories

After Bacon, more "scientific" theories started to fly from the pens of eager theorists. A Frenchman, Etienne Félix Berlioux (1828–1910), claimed in 1874 to have found the ruins of Atlantis at the foot of the mountains on the Moroccan Atlas mountain range near Casablanca. His theory inspired a novel called *L'Atlantide*, by Pierre Benoît (1886–1962), which tells the story of two Frenchmen who find a living Atlantis in the mountains of southern Algeria. The novel was so popular that it was translated into English and published in 1920 under the title *The Queen of Atlantis*. Later, it was made into a movie no less than three times: as a silent film in 1921, as an early "talkie" in Germany in 1932, and in Hollywood in 1949, as the film *Siren of Atlantis*.

In the early part of the twentieth century, Claude Roux, another Frenchman, placed Atlantis in the Mediterranean coast of northwest Africa, which he said at one time was a fertile area. The location, he stated, was invaded so many times that the residents collectively forgot their history and their Atlantean origins.

Meanwhile, Count Byron Kuhn de Prorok felt Atlantis was in the Sahara Desert and claimed to have located traces of it there, including the skeletal remains of

Atlantean Tin Hinan—the main character of Pierre Benoît's novel. Needless to say, it wasn't the fictional Tin Hinan, but only the remains of a local dignitary.

Others felt that they had found Atlantis when they had encountered something else entirely. One such man was Paul Borchardt, a geologist, who discovered the remains of a palace in Tunisia that he claimed were those of Atlantis. It was actually a Roman fortress—a valuable find, but certainly not what he'd anticipated. Albert Herrmann also unearthed ancient irrigation works in Tunisia and wildly theorized that these had to have been part of an Atlantean colony that had come from the Netherlands! Unfortunately for Herrmann, it was not.

Donnelly's Book

One of the most famous Atlantean scholars was not a scientist but a politician with a keen interest in the lost continent. Ignatius Loyola Donnelly (1831–1901), was born in Philadelphia, Pennsylvania, but later moved to Minnesota where he became lieutenant governor and a U.S. congressman and senator. Donnelly published his book *Atlantis: The Antediluvian World* in 1882, after which the study of Atlantis became the talk of the nineteenth-century world. (The word "antediluvian" means before the flood that was described in the Bible.) His theories on Atlantis were extremely imaginative and inspiring, and his book was so well received that for nearly a century, he was considered the primary source on Atlantis, even though those theories have, to put it mildly, very little scientific truth.

Donnelly states that Plato did not invent Atlantis and that his story is historically accurate. Atlantis was exactly where Plato described it, in the mouth of the Mediterranean Sea. There, humans grew to be civilized and colonized regions around the globe, including the Gulf of Mexico, the Mississippi River, the Amazon, the Pacific coast of South America, the Mediterranean, the west coasts of Europe and Africa, the Baltic Sea, the Black Sea, and the Caspian Sea.

Donnelly also believed that Atlantis was paradise. It was the Garden of Eden, the Elysian Fields (the ancient Grecian paradise), Mount Olympus (the home of the gods in Greek legend), and Asgard (the home of the gods in Norse legend), as well as the focal point of many other religious beliefs. There, mankind had been peaceful and happy for generations. In addition, the gods and goddesses of most ancient cultures were the kings, queens, and heroes of Atlantis.

Egypt, Donnelly says, was formed as an Atlantean colony, and Atlantean iron and bronze tools were the first to appear on Earth. The Phoenician

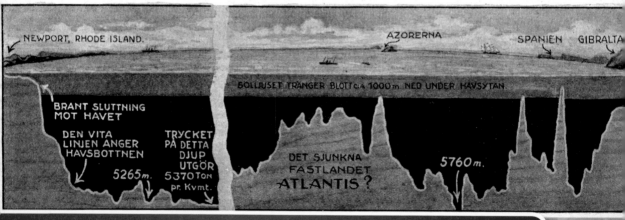

This Dutch print shows the possible elevation of Atlantis and its location beneath the Azores, the islands off the coast of Portugal. Newport, Rhode Island, is at the top, left, and Atlantis is at the bottom, center. Donnelly believed that the Azores were actually the mountain peaks of Atlantis.

alphabet, from which all the European alphabets come, stemmed from an alphabet from Atlantis. The Atlantis alphabet also inspired the alphabet of the Mayans in Central America. The Atlantean race spawned most of the races on Earth. When Atlantis sunk cataclysmically into the ocean, some Atlanteans escaped on ships and rafts and went to other nations telling of the disaster, bringing about the many legends of the Great Flood.

One can see, just by reading Donnelly's theories, why they were so popular. They explain practically every mystery of the ancient world in one fell swoop. In later years, scientists would disprove most of his statements. Geologists have proved, for instance, that Atlantis did not sink into the ocean the way that Donnelly said. Landmasses, although they can sink, take thousands and millions of years to do so. Even the fastest sinking landmasses could not possibly sink as quickly as Plato and Donnelly claim. The only way it could happen, even theoretically, is in a small area no bigger than a few miles (several kilometers) as a result of an earthquake or volcanic eruption. Nothing on the scale of what Plato described would be possible.

Other Theorists

Even so, Donnelly's theories still have a following today and have been the basis for many films, novels, television shows, comic books, and other works of art.

One of Donnelly's fans, Lewis Spence (1874–1955), was one of the most prolific and well-known of the Atlantis scholars. Spence, a news reporter, expounded on his predecessor's theories, stating that an entire continent

DONNELLY'S THIRTEEN PROPOSITIONS

In his book *Atlantis: The Antediluvian World* (1882), Ignatius Donnelly described thirteen propositions about Atlantis. He explained that, first, there once existed a large island in the Atlantic Ocean, opposite the mouth of the Mediterranean, which was what was left of an Atlantic continent, known to the ancients as Atlantis. Second, Plato's description of this island was not fiction, but historical fact. Third, Atlantis was the area where humans first rose from a state of barbarism to civilization. Fourth, after many ages, Atlantis became a populous and mighty nation, whose people migrated to North and South America, Europe, Africa, and other places. Fifth, Atlantis was the Garden of Eden, the Greek Mount Olympus, the Gardens of the Hesperides, the Elysian Fields, and Asgard, and represented "a universal memory of a great land, where early mankind dwelt for ages in peace and happiness." Sixth, the gods and goddesses of the Greeks and other ancients were the kings, queens, and heroes of Atlantis, and the acts credited to them in myths are a confused recollection of actual historical events. Seventh, the mythology of Egypt and Peru represented the original religion of

Atlantis, which was sun worship. Eighth, the oldest colony formed by the Atlanteans was probably in Egypt. Ninth, the Bronze Age tools of Europe were derived from Atlantis, and the Atlanteans were the first manufacturers of iron. Tenth, the Phoenician alphabet originated from the alphabet of Atlantis, which also was transported to the Mayas of Central America. Eleventh, Atlantis was the original seat of the Aryan or Indo-European family of nations, including the Semitic peoples and perhaps the Turanian races. Twelfth, Atlantis vanished in a horrible convulsion of nature, in which the entire island sunk into the ocean, with nearly all its inhabitants. Thirteenth, a few people escaped in ships and on rafts, and carried to nations east and west the stories of its catastrophe, which have survived today in the flood and deluge legends of various nations of the Old and New Worlds.

once spanned America and Europe, and that when it sank, it left several islands in its wake—namely the Canaries, the Azores, Madeira, and the West Indies. He also stated that the people of Atlantis, who begot all the races of the world, were exceptionally tall—a type of master race. Spence, however, hated Nazi Germany, which had risen to power in his time, and stated emphatically that Nazi Germany would fall for the same reason that Atlantis fell—corruption.

Other Atlantean theorists actually paved the way for genuine scientific research with their theories. Although they didn't lead people anywhere closer to Atlantis, they brought to light things about the world that scholars did not know previously.

One example of this was from Professor Pierre Termier of Paris who believed, as many did, that Atlantis had sunk and that its lands lay beneath the Atlantic Ocean. In 1915, he set about describing these lands beneath the ocean from what he knew of the ocean at the time and came surprisingly close to describing exactly what we now refer to as the Mid-Atlantic Ridge of mountains, which was not found until the 1940s. Although modern ocean-ographers know that the Mid-Atlantic Ridge was, and always has been, an underwater mountain range formed by underwater volcanic action and not a sunken continent, Termier had miraculously figured out it was there, without ever seeing it.

Another scientific discovery that came to light from the theories of Atlantis is continental drift, or the fact that the continents move and shift location very slowly, floating like icebergs. Alfred Wegener introduced this theory in 1915 and was summarily laughed at by his peers. Years later, Atlantologists latched onto his ideas, and when other scientists took another hard look at his findings, they realized Wegener was right. Although the Atlantologists proved nothing about Atlantis, they did bring notoriety to a scientific theory that sorely needed it.

Atlantologists still love this theory. In 1995, Rand and Rose Flem-Ath used the premise in their attempt to prove that Atlantis was actually the frozen continent of Antarctica. They theorized that because of continental drift, the sheet of ice drifted over the continent, and it rests there today, buried beneath the ice. Most geologists today consider their hypothesis highly unlikely.

Meanwhile, other theorists have tried to explain the myth of Atlantis. Charles Berlitz (1913–2003), a language teacher and the grandson of the founder of the Berlitz language schools, wrote a book on the Bermuda Triangle and one entitled *Atlantis: The Eighth Continent*, in which he proposed that some of the strange happenings in that area of the Bermuda Triangle might be by-products of the type of event that caused Atlantis to sink beneath the ocean.

Others, such as Immanuel Velikovsky, suggested that Atlantis was destroyed by something greater than a flood or a volcano. Velikovsky was of the opinion that an extraterrestrial event caused destruction on Earth. He believed that Venus, acting as a comet, swung too close to Earth and caused the catastrophic disruption on Earth's surface. Although his ideas were (and still are) considered a bit far-fetched, to say the least, he points to ancient sources that describe similar incidents of ancient volcanic activity in Mayan and Egyptian texts as well as those of the Bible. He also quotes *Timaeus*, in which Plato writes of periods in which the paths of the planets varied and caused widespread destruction on Earth.

If true, such a cataclysmic event would have left an indelible mark on the minds of those who survived it. How is it that someone from that time did not find a way of communicating the story in more detail? Velikovsky explains this away as a form of mass amnesia. The incidents, he says, were too horrible to remember, so the human race simply forgot about it.

How can anyone prove or disprove that?

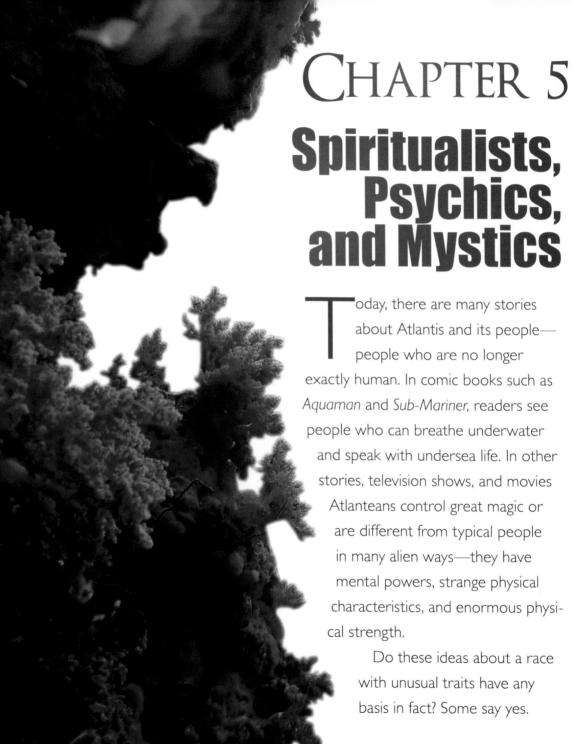

CHAPTER 5

Spiritualists, Psychics, and Mystics

Today, there are many stories about Atlantis and its people—people who are no longer exactly human. In comic books such as *Aquaman* and *Sub-Mariner*, readers see people who can breathe underwater and speak with undersea life. In other stories, television shows, and movies Atlanteans control great magic or are different from typical people in many alien ways—they have mental powers, strange physical characteristics, and enormous physical strength.

Do these ideas about a race with unusual traits have any basis in fact? Some say yes.

DC Comics superhero Aquaman, the son of an Atlantean princess, made his debut in 1941. Some of his superhuman powers are the ability to live in the ocean depths, to breathe underwater, and to swim at very fast speeds.

Ignatius Donnelly started the tradition by writing that Atlantis was the true paradise described by many religions of the world and that many cultures and languages found their origins in Atlantis.

The Fourth Race

One of the earliest Atlantis spiritualists was Madame Helena Blavatsky. After coming to New York City in 1871, Madame Blavatsky gained a great following in the last twenty years of the nineteenth century, claiming that her spiritual adviser, Koot Hoomie, a Hindu master, sent her letters telling her about an ancient history of the world. (It was later discovered that she was writing them to herself.) Madame Blavatsky promoted the belief that there were many ancient "root" races on Earth, one of which was the Atlanteans. Atlanteans, she claimed, were the fourth race of man, who were preceded by the third race, the Lemurians—who were 15 feet (4.6 meters) tall. They had eyes so far apart that they could see sideways, and their heels were so long that they could walk backward as well as forward. Humans, Blavatsky believed, are the fifth race of man on Earth.

Visions and Spirits

Some of the most interesting mystical looks at Atlantis come by way of psychics. There have been many mystics over the years who have claimed a "psychic" connection to Atlantis. One such psychic, Dion Fortune (1890–1946), claimed that she saw Atlantis in a vision when she was only four years old. After she died, another psychic, Gareth Knight (1930–), stated that he learned about Atlantis from Dion Fortune, who'd visited him as a spirit. Knight confirmed that the Atlanteans were a different race from humans and that they were 7 feet (2.1 m) tall and had a soft, spongelike quality to their skin. Christine Hartley, a psychic who worked extensively on the belief in reincarnation, believed that Atlanteans grew so much in intelligence and mental powers that they outgrew their moral development.

Edgar Cayce and His Fans

Most of these psychics claimed to be channeling spirits from Atlantis, or receiving their information from the world beyond. Edgar Cayce, one of the most famous psychics of the twentieth century, was no exception. Cayce put himself into hypnotic trances, and in this state, he'd communicate all that he was learning from the spirit world. Born in 1877, Cayce learned of this ability as a youth when he had a throat illness that caused him to lose his voice. A friend offered to cure him by putting him in a hypnotic trance, and under hypnosis, Cayce was able to speak normally. As he grew older, he treated people by putting them in hypnotic trances and prescribing treatments. He claimed to be able read a person's "aura," or halo of energy around the person's body, and diagnose ailments from it. He became known around the country for his miraculous cures.

In his trances, Cayce stated he could see into the past and predict the future. He predicted the destruction of Los Angeles, San Francisco, and New York, the conversion of China to democracy, the destruction of Japan (sliding into the sea), and the end of Communism in Russia. All of this was to happen

Edgar Cayce, an American faith healer and psychic, supported the belief in the existence of Atlantis. While in a self-induced trance, Cayce channeled answers to questions on a variety of topics, including whether Atlanteans' descendants were the Egyptians and Mayans.

before 1998. Although only the last prediction has come to pass, many believed him—especially when it came to Atlantis.

Cayce studied 1,600 people, and from the psychic "life readings" of those people, he predicted the reemergence of Atlantis. Apparently half of the people were, in his opinion, reincarnated citizens of the fabled lost continent. He believed that the souls of Atlantis were returning to Earth to bring about great change. When in a tracelike state, he would hear the words of these reincarnated souls and have them transcribed. From these transcriptions, he revealed what happened to Atlantis, according to those who lived there.

According to these ancient spirits, the world at the time of Atlantis was topsy-turvy—the northern portion of Earth was the southern portion. The Nile opened into the Atlantic Ocean, and the Sahara was a fertile land. That the Sahara was once fertile is fact; experts have no geologic evidence to back up the rest of Cayce's claims.

Cayce passed away in 1945. But before he died, he revealed what the spirits told him—the exact location of the fabled lost continent. Atlantis, Cayce stated, was between the Gulf of Mexico and the Mediterranean, and the British West Indies or the Bahamas are what remain of it. In fact, he placed it near Bimini, in the Bahamas. Cayce stated that a great cataclysm destroyed Atlantis, a civilization so technologically advanced that it harnessed atomic energy and invented flying machines fifty thousand years ago. Survivors of the destruction spread across the world and gave their achievements to ancient civilizations such as the Egyptians. He said they buried their most important documents under the paws of the Sphinx in Egypt.

THE GREAT CRYSTAL

During his informational "readings" after going into trances, Edgar Cayce often described an instrument, the Great Crystal, which the Atlanteans used to obtain energy from the sun. He claimed that it was housed in an oval building, which had a dome that could be rolled back to expose the Great Crystal to the light of the sun, moon, and stars. The crystal, a six-sided prism, was gigantic and cylindrical in shape. At the top was a movable capstone that was used to concentrate incoming rays of energy and direct them to specific areas of Atlantis. In time, the Atlanteans used the energy currents to revitalize their bodies so that they could live hundreds of years and sustain their youthful looks. Eventually, the Atlanteans used the Great Crystal to transmit energy similar to radio waves to power various vehicles at fast speeds in the sky and under the sea.

Based on what he said the souls of Atlantis told him, Cayce predicted that Atlantis would rise again around the year 1968. Hearing this prophesy, several people mounted expeditions to the Bahamas to look in the areas Cayce had indicated, waiting for the fabled land to rise. Two of his followers were Robert Ferro and Michael Grumley, who located an underwater grouping of geometrically shaped rocks near the coast of Bimini that they felt was proof of an underwater city. Sadly, these two gentlemen claimed their inspiration through the questionable influences of tarot cards and marijuana, so their findings were suspect.

Following up on their apparent discovery, David Zink, another one of Cayce's enthusiasts and an expert scuba diver, organized three expeditions, in 1975, 1976, and 1977, in which he dived over and photographed the stones in question. He claimed they had the appearance of buildings, and one could almost see "streets" in the way they were laying along the seabed. He declared they were columns and that they showed the definite remains of a lost civilization.

After studying the stones, however, oceanologists and geologists explained that it is not unusual for undersea stone formations near beach rock to break in straight lines and right angles, giving the appearance of buildings. These rocks, as it turns out, are really shaped naturally based on the environment and are not the fabled Atlantis ruins rising from the sea.

In 1967, shortly before Cayce's followers were turning the Bahamas upside down searching for proof of Atlantis's resurrection, Greek archaeologist Spyridon Marinatos (1901–1974) began excavating on a volcanic island in the Mediterranean. There he uncovered the capital of an ancient civilization that made all Atlantean scholars and researchers take notice. Had Atlantis truly risen again—on the island of Santorini?

CHAPTER 6

The Minoans, Plato's Atlanteans?

After all of the wild theories, most of which are based on decidedly shaky evidence, modern science may have found a clue in the search for Atlantis. Study of the legend has centered on the Greek islands of Crete and Santorini in the Sea of Crete (a sea where the Aegean Sea and the Mediterranean Sea meet). Santorini, also called Santorin and Thera, is the southernmost island of the Cyclades group. It is a semi-circular island, all that remains of an exploded volcano—a volcano that reputedly erupted around the year 1645 BCE. Separated by only 60 miles (97 km), the islands of

This Minoan mural from the Palace of Knossos on Crete depicts a king or priest with lilies. Many scientists believe that the volcanic eruption on Santorini caused a tsunami that contributed to the collapse of the Minoan civilization.

Crete and Thera/Santorini housed a mysterious ancient people that archaeologists now refer to as the Minoans.

About 2,500 years ago, this extremely powerful and successful culture
ruled the region. Threatened only by their aggressive Greek neighbors, the
Mycenaeans, they remained solidly rooted for a thousand years.

What's really strange about this people, is how suddenly they appeared as
if from nowhere and how suddenly they disappeared. Archaeologists in the
latter half of the twentieth century uncovered more clues about them and
their sudden disappearance and found possible links between them and Plato's
tale of Atlantis.

Eight thousand years ago, the first settlers of Crete arrived on the
island's shores. Archaeologists have uncovered their remains and have found
them to be a small and slender people, very similar to the people of the
Mediterranean today. Archaeologists also found remains of a different people,
however, a taller and shorter-skulled race, which apparently joined the previous population of Crete around 2500 BCE with little or no violence.

Thera's Eruption

In 1866, on the island of Santorini, a French volcanologist, Ferdinand Foqué,
was studying the volcano that had erupted there and caught word of two
mysterious tombs hidden in the hardened lava. Enlisting the aid of some
archaeologists, he uncovered the first Minoan remains to come to light for
2,500 years—he found a crypt with a central pillar made of blocks of lava,
human skeletons, blades made of obsidian, and pottery that was decorated

This twentieth-century painting shows people fleeing across the Aegean Sea during the eruption of Thera on Santorini. Some experts believe that Atlanteans who escaped the destruction of Atlantis traveled to various continents and took their advanced culture with them.

in a style no one had seen before. After some study, he found that a volcanic eruption around 2000 BCE had blown the island apart—separating it into three islands that remain in the Santorini group of islands today. His research showed that a volcanic eruption of this magnitude would have been heard as far as away as Gibraltar, Scandinavia, the Arabian Sea, and Central Africa. It would have created tsunami tidal waves of mythic proportion, sending them crashing down on the nearby islands, including the island of Crete, and would have rocked them with earthquakes, darkening the sky and smothering them with volcanic ash.

An example of how large a tidal wave a volcano can create was witnessed in 1883, with the volcano Krakatau, or Krakatoa, which sent 135-foot (41-meter) waves to the nearby coasts of Java and Sumatra, flooding nearly three hundred towns and villages and drowning almost thirty-six thousand people.

Palace of King Minos

Realizing that Foqué's team had discovered a civilization older than that of the Mycenaeans, a British archaeologist named Arthur Evans (1851–1941) went to Crete to see if he could find more evidence of this culture on the other island. On Crete, Evans uncovered a huge palace, which he believed to be the home of King Minos, the legendary ruler of Crete in Greek mythology. In honor of King Minos, he named the ancient race of people who had built that palace and the surrounding area settlement Minoans. Study of the palace showed that it had been severely damaged by earthquakes and other natural disasters.

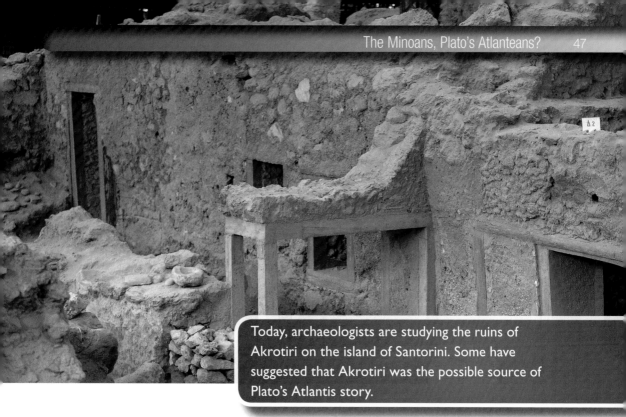

Today, archaeologists are studying the ruins of Akrotiri on the island of Santorini. Some have suggested that Akrotiri was the possible source of Plato's Atlantis story.

After these disasters greatly weakened the Minoans, scientists believe the Mycenaeans invaded Minoan territory, claiming it for their own.

Akrotiri

In 1967, Spyridon Marinatos, a Greek archaeologist, decided to dig in a part of Santorini known as Akrotiri. In 1939, he had theorized that the eruption of Thera was the inspiration for the legend of Atlantis. He chose Akrotiri to further explore this theory, and there he uncovered multileveled buildings, as well as a high level of culture and art that was greater in size than what had been found by the earlier archaeological work on Crete and Santorini.

THE CASE FOR THE ISLAND OF CYPRUS

In 2004, the Iranian American architect Robert Sarmast announced that he had discovered the legendary Atlantis. Using sonar equipment and scanning technology, he claimed that he found man-made walls similar to those of Atlantis as described by Plato. The location of the site was between Cyprus and Syria in the Mediterranean Sea. Sarmast contends that Cyprus was a bigger island once and that Atlantis was situated on the portion of the island that is presently under the Mediterranean. He also theorizes that Atlantis and the Garden of Eden are the same place. After founding his own research company (see Discovery of Atlantis at http://www.discoveryofatlantis.com), Sarmast went on additional expeditions in the area near Cyprus. In 2007, a geologist determined that some of the structures beneath the ocean that Sarmast believed were Atlantean buildings were actually underwater formations of floor sediments. Sarmast continues to raise funding for further research in the region around Cyprus to support his theories and findings.

Akrotiri, Marinatos believed, was the real capital of the Minoan civilization because of the incredible palaces they'd uncovered and the expanse of the settlement. What was most amazing about the find was that it confirmed that this location was completely leveled by a volcano, and it focused the time period of the event at or around the year 1500 BCE, exactly 1,000 years after the Minoans appeared on Crete.

The Mysterious Minoans

The language of the Minoans, it was discovered, was an early form of Greek. Although two classical scholars named John Chadwick (1920–1998) and Michael Ventris (1922–1956) managed to decipher some of it, scholars have none of the Minoans' stories, histories, or literature. They do not even know what the Minoans called themselves, for all the items available for translation were simple lists and ledgers. Nothing else was written down, at least not on materials that lasted. For this reason, the Minoans remain a nameless, mysterious, brilliant people, a people who were once a world power.

Could these elusive people, this great nation, be the origin for Plato's story? Only further scientific study will tell the tale. Although the time period does not match Plato's story, surely a great civilization such as the one found on Crete and Santorini could have posed a threat to the ancient Greeks as Plato proposed—and its cataclysmic death could have inspired his story. Scholars may never know the truth. Atlantis hides its secrets very well. But no doubt, the mystery and glamour of the story will inspire many others to search for the tragic, fabled land. Someday, one of them just may find it.

CHAPTER 7

Atlantis in Art and Literature

Atlantis has been featured in many books, films, and television programs throughout history. It has become an important part of pop culture.

Novels

In French author Jules Verne's classic science fiction novel, *Twenty Thousand Leagues Under the Sea* (1870), Captain Nemo and Professor Pierre Aronnax visit the ruins of Atlantis in Nemo's submarine, the *Nautilus*. In Chapter IX, "A Vanished Continent," Aronnax describes the scene he has just encountered:

There indeed under my eyes, ruined, destroyed, lay a town—its roofs open to the sky, its temples fallen, its arches dislocated, its columns lying on the ground, from which one would still recognize the massive character of Tuscan architecture. Further on, some remains of a gigantic aqueduct; here the high base of an Acropolis, with the floating outline of a Parthenon … Where was I? … I tried to speak, but Captain Nemo stopped me by a gesture, and, picking up a piece of chalk-stone, advanced to a rock of black basalt, and traced the one word: ATLANTIS.

In his science fiction novel *The Maracot Deep* (1929), Sir Arthur Conan Doyle writes about the discovery of the submerged city of Atlantis by a group of explorers whose leader is Professor Maracot. The scientific team takes a submersible to the seabed of the Atlantic and explores the deep trenches off the coast of Africa. As the team encounters the sunken world, a giant crustacean severs their line and throws them down into the trench. Within the depths of the trench, the team is saved by the Atlanteans, who are the only survivors of the land that once was Atlantis:

We saw it in our mind's eye stretched out, over miles of what was now the bed of the Atlantic, the shattered city lying alongside of the ark or refuges in which the handful of nerve-shattered survivors were assembled. And then finally we understood how these had carried on their lives, how they had used the various devices with which the foresight and science of their great leader had endowed them, how he had

This illustration is from Jules Verne's novel *Twenty Thousand Leagues Under the Sea*, which was published in 1870. The scene depicts Captain Nemo and Professor Aronnax's visit to the lost city of Atlantis.

taught them all his arts before he passed away, and how some fifty or sixty survivors had grown now into a large community, which had to dig its way into the bowels of the earth in order to get room to expand.

In *The Magician's Nephew* (1955), the sixth book in *The Chronicles of Narnia* series, C. S. Lewis writes about a box that a character, Digory Kirke's uncle Andrew, received and that has Atlantean symbols. The box from Atlantis contains the dust from which Andrew Ketterley creates the rings Digory and Polly use to travel between worlds. Lewis's friend J. R. R. Tolkien also used the Atlantis legend in his book, *The Silmarillion*, which includes the *Akallabêth* of Atlantë, the history of his adaptation of Atlantis, known as the Island of Númenóreans. Númenor was the home of the most advanced civilization of men in the history of Middle-earth, and, much like Atlantis, the Island of Númenor was swallowed into the sea in a single night.

Other writers and novelists who have referred to Atlantis in their works include Edgar Rice Burroughs in his Tarzan series (*The Return of Tarzan* [1913], *The Jewels of Opar* [1916], *Tarzan and the Golden Lion* [1923], and *Tarzan the Invincible* [1930]), which describes a colony of Atlantis, the lost city of Opar. Diane Duane's fantasy novel, *Deep Wizardry* (1985), the second book in her Young Wizards series, explains how the downfall of Atlantis was triggered by the failure of an ancient wizardry meant to preserve the balance of Earth and the sea. Stephen King uses the lost civilization of Atlantis as a metaphor for the ideals and aspirations of popular culture in the 1960s in his book *Hearts in Atlantis* (1966). King investigates how university life was a kind of

Atlantis, an imaginary kingdom that was isolated from the challenges of the real world, how young male students avoided serving in the military during the Vietnam War, and how students became addicted to playing the game of Hearts instead. Their college grades suffered because of that, and therefore the students jeopardized their military deferments by risking their safety net of college if they failed courses.

Films

The legend of Atlantis has provided lots of creative ideas for film and moviemakers over the years. Jules Verne's 1864 novel *Journey to the Center of the Earth* was made into a film in 1959 and a sort of 3-D sequel in 2008. Explorers try to reach Earth's core and come upon the remnants of Atlantis, which are located deep within the planet. In the 2008 movie, the characters Trevor, a volcanologist, Sean, his nephew, and Hannah, the daughter of another volcanologist who they are visiting in Iceland, fall into a volcanic tube that takes them to the center of Earth and drops them into a lake. Near the end of the film, as a friendly gesture, the character Trevor hands Sean a copy of Ignatius Donnelly's book *Atlantis: The Antediluvian World*.

Cocoon (1985), a science fiction film directed by Ron Howard, is about a group of four aliens from the planet Antarea who return to Earth to find twenty of their species who were left behind when Atlantis was abandoned some ten thousand years earlier. Atlantis supposedly sank because of an earthquake, and the twenty members were left behind so that the others could return to their home planet. The Antareans, who disguise themselves as

THE KING OF ATLANTIS

Einar Jónsson (1873–1954) was a sculptor who lived in Iceland and is considered to be one of the country's most renowned sculptors. Many of the subjects he portrayed are taken from Nordic mythology, Icelandic folklore, and the Bible. In 1919, he began his work, *King of Atlantis*, a bronze sculpture. Jónsson completed the piece in 1922, which is now located in the sculpture garden of the Einar Jónsson Museum in Reykjavik, Iceland.

humans, finally have returned to pick up their abandoned comrades. The Antareans, though, have to retrieve cocoons, which help them sustain their life force, from the ruins of Atlantis so that they can return to their home planet. In 1985, a sequel, *Cocoon: The Return*, picks up the story, with the Antareans returning to Earth to rescue the cocoons that they had to leave behind.

Disney Studios has relied on the Atlantis legend for some of its animated films, including *The Little Mermaid* (1989), and the character Atlantica in *Atlantis: The Lost Empire* (2001) and *Atlantis: Milo's Return* (2003). The Atlantis films have been influenced by Edgar Cayce's ideas, including the ships and aircraft that were powered by the energy currents from the Great Crystal.

On the bridge of the submarine *The Ulysses*, the explorers in Disney's animated film *Atlantis: The Lost Empire* (2001) encounter the undersea world during their voyage to Atlantis.

Television

A television series called *Man from Atlantis* appeared for thirteen episodes on the NBC network in 1977–78. The main character of the series, Mark Harris, was an amnesiac who supposedly was a survivor of Atlantis. He could breathe underwater, subsist in the high pressures of the deepest depths of the ocean, and had superhuman strength. His hands and feet were webbed, and when he swam, his motions were similar to marine mammals that had flippers.

One of the biggest Atlantis-themed successes on TV has been *Stargate Atlantis*. This Canadian-American science fiction series was a spin-off series of *Stargate SG-1*, which was based on the movie *Stargate* (1994). The series first appeared in 2004 on the Sci-Fi Channel and the Movie Network. The final two seasons aired only on the Sci-Fi Channel, the last episode being broadcast in 2009. The storyline follows the cast's characters, who have discovered an alien race's outpost that has been founded in Antarctica. The team discovers that the alien race, called Ancients, created the legendary city, Atlantis.

Anime

In the Japanese-French animated series *The Mysterious Cities of Gold* (also known as *Esteban, A Boy from the Sun*), which debuted in Japan in 1982 and ran for thirty-nine episodes, until 1983, the adventures of Esteban, a young Spaniard are portrayed. Taking place in 1532, the series follows Esteban, Zia, an Incan girl, and Tao, the last survivor of Mu, on a voyage to the New World to search for Esteban's father and the lost Cities of Gold. The series combines ancient South American history, science fiction, and archaeology. The characters meet the Mayas, Incas, and Olmecs during their trip. They also stumble on many technological marvels of the Mu Empire, including *Solaris*,

In this scene from the episode "Sateda" in the third season of the Sci-Fi series *Stargate Atlantis*, the Wraith leader *(left)* and Ronan Dex fight on the planet Sateda. Supposedly the TV series was loosely based on ancient Greek stories of the lost city of Atlantis.

a solar-powered ship, and the Golden Condor, a solar-powered mechanical bird. The Emperor of Mu built the Seven Cities of Gold out of fear of a possible war that could destroy the world. A previous war had occurred, which destroyed the Mu Empire and Atlantis. In the end, Esteban's father is killed in a nuclearlike accident, by replacing Tao's jar, the cooling or control rod system for the Great Legacy, thus saving the others.

Comics

DC Comics and Marvel Comics have several characters and locations that have been influenced by the Atlantis legend. The DC Comic superhero Aquaman and Lori Lemaris, a mermaid, supposedly came from the lost continent of Atlantis. They can survive by breathing water. Some Atlantean civilizations in the DC Universe include Poseidonis, the home of Aquaman, and Tritonis, home of Lemaris. In the 1990s, Aquaman's character assumed the kingship of Atlantis and all its weighty concerns.

In the Ultimate Marvel comics, Atlantis was the land of a technologically superior civilization. It was sunk by space gods, the Celestials. Eventually the sunken Atlantis was populated by the genetic offshoot of humans, called *Homo mermanus*, including Namor the Sub-Mariner. These people can breathe underwater and have mighty technologies.

The legend of Atlantis attracts people who are interested in ancient history and mythology. Its legacy continues to grow in pop culture today and in people's never-ending interest in fantasy and their shared imagination that it could be an actual place waiting, anxiously, to be substantiated by fact!

GLOSSARY

archaeology The scientific study of ancient cultures through the examination of their material remains, such as buildings, graves, tools, and other artifacts usually dug up from the ground.

Atlantean A person who resides in Atlantis.

cataclysm A sudden and violent upheaval or disaster that causes great changes in society.

concentric Something with a common middle point, such as circles of different sizes with the same middle point.

continental drift The gradual movement of the continents across Earth's surface through geological time.

demise The end of something that used to exist, especially when it happens slowly and predictably; the death of someone.

elusive Difficult to understand, define, or identify.

idyllic Extremely happy, peaceful, or picturesque.

mystic Someone who practices or believes in mysticism, which is the belief that personal communication or union with the divine is achieved through intuition, faith, ecstasy, or sudden insight, rather than through rational thought.

psychic A person considered or claiming to have psychic powers; a medium.

theology The study of the nature of God and religious belief.

trilogy A group of three related novels, plays, films, operas, or albums. In ancient Greece, it was a series of three tragedies performed one after the other.

FOR MORE INFORMATION

American Museum of Natural History

Central Park West at 79th Street

New York, NY 10024-5192

(212) 769-5001

Web site: http://www.amnh.org

The museum contains numerous artifacts and displays them, including collections about ancient Greece and Rome. Experts in anthropology, geology, biodiversity, evolution, conservation, paleontology, astronomy, cultural history, and archaeology provide guidance and information about various programs and exhibits.

Archaeological Institute of America

Boston University

656 Beacon Street, 6th Floor

Boston, MA 02215-2006

(617) 353-9361

Web site: http://www.archaeological.org

The institute is devoted to the world of archaeology. It promotes the discovery and understanding of material records of human history around the world.

Canadian Archaeological Association (CAA)

c/o Department of Archaeology

Simon Fraser University

Burnaby, BC V5I 1S6

Canada

(604) 258-7521

Web site: http://www.canadianarchaeology.com

The CAA educates Canadians about archaeological knowledge and partici-
pates with many groups in studying First Peoples' heritage.

Metropolitan Museum of Art (MMA)

1000 Fifth Avenue

New York, NY 10028-0198

(212) 535-7710

Web site: http://www.metmuseum.org

One of the world's largest museums, the MMA has more than two million
works of art spanning prehistory to the present.

Web Sites

Due to the changing nature of Internet links, Rosen Publishing has developed
an online list of Web sites related to the subject of this book. This site is
updated regularly. Please use this link to access the list:

http://www.rosenlinks.com/me/atl

FOR FURTHER READING

Berlitz, Charles. *Atlantis: The Eighth Continent*. New York, NY: Fawcett, 1985.

Cayce, Edgar Evans. *Edgar Evans on Atlantis*. New York, NY: Warner Books, 1999.

Collins, Andrew. *Gateway to Atlantis: The Search for the Source of a Lost Civilization*. New York, NY: Basic Books, 2002.

DeCamp, L. Sprague. *Lost Continents: The Atlantis Theme in History, Science, and Literature*. New York, NY: Dover, 1970.

Donnelly, Ignatius. *Atlantis: The Antediluvian World*. London, England: The British Library, 2010.

Ellis, Richard. *Imagining Atlantis*. New York, NY: Vintage Books, 1999.

Frazee, Charles. *Atlantis* (Ancient Greek Mystery Series). Provo, UT: Artesian Press, 2007.

Joseph, Frank. *Atlantis and 2012: The Science of the Lost Civilization and the Prophecies of the Maya*. Rochester, VT: Bear & Company, 2010.

Joseph, Frank. *Atlantis Encyclopedia*. Pompton Plains, NJ: Career Press, 2008.

Joseph, Frank. *The Destruction of Atlantis: Compelling Evidence of the Sudden Fall of the Legendary Civilization*. Rochester, VT: Bear & Company, 2004.

Luce, J. V. *Lost Atlantis: New Light on an Old Legend*. London, England: Thames & Hudson, 1969.

Nardo, Don. *Atlantis* (The Mystery Library). Farmington Hills, MI: Lucent Books, 2004.

Plato. *Timaeus and Critias*. Seattle, WA: CreateSpace, 2009.

INDEX

About the Authors

Barbara A. Woyt is a writer who lives in New York, New York.

Ann Lewis received her B.A. degree in English literature from Michigan State University in East Lansing. She has written numerous children's stories, comic stories, and activity books for DC Comics. She has contributed to several media magazines, books, and Web sites, and has published a second edition of her book, *Star Wars: The New Essential Guide to Alien Species*. Lewis and her husband and son live in Indianapolis, Indiana.

Photo Credits

Cover, back cover, pp. 1, 6, 8, 10, 12, 14–15, 17, 18, 21, 22–23, 24, 26–27, 29, 30–31, 32–33, 34, 36–37, 39, 40–41, 42, 44, 46, 48–49, 50, 51, 53, 54–55, 58, 64 Shutterstock; cover, back cover, p. 1 (camera lens) © www.istockphoto.com/jsemeniuk; pp. 4–5 Hemera/Thinkstock; pp. 7, 47 De Agostini Picture Library/Getty Images; p. 9 InterNetwork Media/Digital Vision/Getty Images; p. 11 © akg-images/Peter Connolly/The Image Works; pp. 13, 43 The Bridgeman Art Library/Getty Images; p. 16 Henry Guttmann/Hulton Archive/Getty Images; pp. 19, 25 © 2003 Charles Walker/Topfoto/The Image Works; p. 20 iStockphoto/Thinkstock; p. 28 © Mary Evans Picture Library/The Image Works; p. 35 © DC Comics/Everett Collection; p. 38 Apic/Getty Images; p. 45 Lloyd Kenneth Townsend, Jr./National Geographic/Getty Images; p. 52 © Photo12/The Image Works; p. 56 © Buena Vista Pictures/Everett Collection; p. 57 Carole Segal/ © MGM Television/Everett Collection.

Designer: Matthew Cauli; Photo Researcher: Amy Feinberg